The Little
Book of
Breathing

This book is dedicated to my mother,
Ruth, who gave me my first breath and
taught me (much later!) about the
health benefits of mindful breathing.

The Little Book of Breathing

Simple practices for connecting with your breath

Una L Tudor

An Hachette UK Company
www.hachette.co.uk

First published in Great Britain in 2019 by Gaia Books,
an imprint of Octopus Publishing Group Ltd
Carmelite House
50 Victoria Embankment
London EC4Y 0DZ
www.octopusbooks.co.uk

Distributed in the US by Hachette Book Group,
1290 Avenue of the Americas, 4th and 5th Floors, New York, NY 10104

Distributed in Canada by Canadian Manda Group
664 Annette Street, Toronto, Ontario, Canada M6S 2C8

ISBN 978-1-85675-396-8

A CIP catalogue record for this book is available from the British Library.

Printed and bound in China.

10 9 8 7 6 5 4 3 2 1

Publishing Director: Stephanie Jackson
Art Director: Juliette Norsworthy
Junior Editor: Sarah Vaughan
Designer and Illustrator: Abi Read
Copy Editor: Clare Churly
Production Controller: Grace O'Byrne

Contents

Introduction

At first glance, the idea of a guide to breathing might seem a little silly. I know, I know: who needs a book to teach them how to breathe? After all, it's a pretty safe bet that you're breathing right now; and until you read this sentence, you weren't even thinking about it. Breathing is automatic, or should be. The average person takes 720 breaths an hour: that's 17,280 breaths a day and 6,307,200 breaths per year! And you took every single one of those breaths without the help of a little guide. So why do you need this book?

Breathing is perhaps the biological process to which we pay the least attention – but it's the most fundamental. Breath is life, after all, and so this book is the answer to a single radical question: what if changing the way we breathe can change the way we live?

What if, simply by considering our breath, we could live more considered, thoughtful lives?

Your Inner World

How can you begin to pay attention to the world around you if you don't pay attention to the world inside you?

The physical body is an amazing thing: a machine that works tirelessly, converting energy to matter and matter to energy. Every second, you are alive with electricity. Your brain sends thousands of signals to your nerves, your muscles expand and contract based only on the tiniest impulses, your bone marrow churns out thousands of blood cells and a thousand neurons leap and whirr together. Your body is an unlikely, astounding miracle that is fuelled by oxygen.

You can survive for three weeks without food, three days without water and barely three *minutes* without oxygen. We pay attention to what we eat and how much we drink, but often we don't stop to consider how we breathe.

How Do You Breathe?

Noticing and controlling our breathing sits in the overlapping section of a Venn diagram between mindfulness and yoga, between science and the spiritual, and chiefly between high-minded theory and practical solutions. You don't have to read any scientific studies or believe in any sacred texts to understand that breathing deeply can help you feel better – or that hyperventilating can make you feel worse.

Everyone knows the wisdom inherent in being told to "take a deep breath", and everyone knows how horrible it feels to be breathless. Focussing on your breath is a kind of applied mindfulness. Where better to start the process of understanding your own presence in the world than with the air you breathe in and out every moment?

Take a little time to try the exercise on the following page. Do it right now, wherever you are.

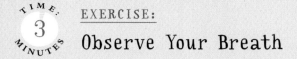

TIME: 3 MINUTES

EXERCISE:

Observe Your Breath

Use this exercise to focus your breath. This will come in handy throughout the rest of the book!

1 Stand or sit comfortably, with your shoulders back.

2 Be as still as you can.

3 Breathe normally.

4 Observe your breath without judgment. Don't try to change it or modulate it. All you're doing for this first exercise is observing your natural state. This is about noticing your "normal". It is about being mindful of every breath you put into the world.

5 Ask yourself:

- *How does the breath feel in my mouth and nose? How about in my chest?*

- *How does the breath feel in my lungs? Is it reaching every part of my lungs or just the top?*

- *How does the breath feel in my throat? Is it cold or hot? Does it hurt at all?*

- *How does my body feel when I breathe in?*

- *How does my body feel when I breathe out?*

6 Take mental note of anything that doesn't seem right.

The Art of Breathing

You've probably noticed that your breathing is a bit uneven – some breaths are slower and others are faster. Sometimes it might take an extra second for you to inhale or exhale, or perhaps even more. It's easy to see how this kind of ragged breath can contribute to a sense that life itself is a little ragged, and how if we can modulate our breath, we can modulate our sense of how our lives are passing too.

Breathing – unlike many forms of complementary therapy – requires no special equipment or space. All you need is the willingness to turn your attention inward for a moment or two.

This book draws on everything from sacred yogic practices and theories of mindfulness (both ancient and modern) to psychological and scientific studies. As you read this guide, you'll realize that many of these techniques are simply practical, everyday remedies for practical, everyday problems.

It seems that in many ways, the art of breathing is really just scientifically sound common sense.

Whether you're religious or not, the words of this time-honoured prayer hold a certain immutable truth:

God grant me

*the **serenity** to accept the
things I cannot change,*

*the **courage** to change the
things I can, and*

*the **wisdom** to know the
difference.*

Change the Way You Breathe

Like life, our breath can seem random, irregular and jumpy, but in a chaotic and unruly world, often our breath is the only thing over which we truly have control. There's so much we can't change, but one thing we can is our breath.

Remember the Observe Your Breath exercise on page 10 and consider what felt good to you in your breath. What didn't feel so good? Was the air reaching every part of your lungs? What about your diaphragm? Were your breaths even and steady?

With the next exercise, you're going to try to modulate those breaths. This technique is based on an ancient yogic exercise called *samavrtti*, which means "same action".

You're simply going to try to make your "inhale" the same as your "exhale". Hopefully, you will feel a little calmer after the exercise, and you'll begin to see why paying attention to the way you breathe can be so important!

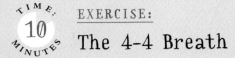

TIME: 10 MINUTES

EXERCISE:

The 4-4 Breath

If all else feels out of control, try practising this exercise to regulate your breathing.

1 Sit or lie down comfortably. Take a minute to settle yourself.

2 Place your hands on the bottom of your ribcage – you should be able to feel the base of your ribs under your palms. Breathe in and out normally, noticing your breath as before (see Observe Your Breath on page 10).

3 After a minute, try to even out those breaths. It can help to start a count in your head: in–two–three–four, out–two–three–four. Count evenly and reasonably slowly.

4 Try to keep your in–breaths even and steady, so that each beat of the inhale is exactly like the other three beats – not one whoosh at the start. Really focus on keeping your breaths steady and coherent. Check that your

shoulders are rising and falling evenly. You should be able to feel your ribs moving under your hands. Try to really breathe *into* your hands, expanding and contracting your lungs. Are you breathing into every part of your lungs?

5 Have you ever heard the phrase "work smarter, not harder"? You're not trying to breathe *more* air, you're trying to make your usual volume of air fill your lungs *properly*, instead of just settling with the front and centre. This can be hard at first, so don't worry if it takes you a little time to get it right, and don't worry if some breaths are still a little long or short. Continue to breathe like this for ten minutes, counting the whole time inside your head.

6 After 10 minutes – or longer if you can, ask yourself:

🪶 *How does the breath feel in my mouth and nose? How about in my chest? My lungs?*

🪶 *How does my body feel when I breathe in?*

🪶 *How does my body feel when I breathe out?*

🪶 *How do I feel for having spent this time with my breath?*

Take Better Care of Yourself

The chapters of this book are arranged around the clock, with breathing techniques suitable for different times of the day, although that doesn't mean you can't dip in and out of the book as you need to.

Some of the techniques are so easy you can do them right where you are, others take a little while to master. Some take as little as a minute and will lend you clarity and energy, while others can be extended to form part of a meditative practice, an immense sense of calm that will allow you to overcome anxiety, stress, panic and even pain.

Whoever you are and however much time you have, conscious breathing can help make your life happier, calmer and smarter. It will allow you to make better decisions, care for yourself physically and mentally, sleep more deeply and be mindful of yourself, your loved ones, your world and your life.

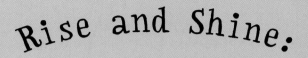

Rise and Shine:

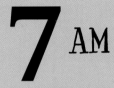

7 AM

We're all familiar with those groggy Monday morning awakenings, but what if there was something you could do to make them easier? What if there was something you could do that would make not just your morning better but your whole day too? What if, instead of rushing about, frantically ironing a shirt with some hair straighteners and scarfing down a banana, you could have the kind of mornings you've always imagined?

In this chapter, we'll look at three exercises to help you get to where you want to be, starting with a very simple morning analysis.

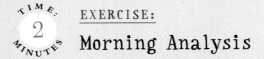

EXERCISE:

Morning Analysis

This exercise will help you to realize your typical morning routine and how it compares with what you'd like it to be (see Visualize Your Perfect Morning on page 23).

1 Using paper and a pen, jot down the basic facts of your average weekday morning. Be as honest as you can be! Ask yourself:

    🔥 *When do you get up?*

    🔥 *When do you need to leave home?*

    🔥 *Do you eat breakfast?*

    🔥 *Do you have time to shower?*

2 Don't forget to ask yourself more searching questions too:

🌿 *What's on your mind when you awake?*

🌿 *How do you feel when you wake up?*

🌿 *How do you feel by the time you leave home?*

🌿 *Do you find yourself rushing?*

🌿 *Do you often feel like you've forgotten something or had to sacrifice something you wanted to do (like having a coffee or brushing your hair) in favour of getting out the door on time?*

🌿 *How do you feel by the time you start your day?*

3 This exercise can be totally free-form – don't be afraid to get creative! It may be a good idea to draw a little timetable. Realistically, where are you at 6:30am, 7:15am, 8:45am? How do you feel at those points on your average day?

Seek Change

Review the notes you jotted down for the Morning Analysis (see page 20). Chances are, you've written something like "frantic", "chaotic" or "stressful" somewhere on the piece of paper, and if so, you're not alone.

The infuriating alarm clock is a cliché for a reason. For example, more than half of Americans[1] wake up thinking about work and finance – and it's fair to think that this might be representative of a global problem. Given that money and work are two leading causes of stress, this can't be good for us. So how do we change things?

Well, we do it the same way we change anything: by working out where we are right now, where we'd like to be and then the difference between the two.

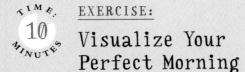

EXERCISE:

Visualize Your Perfect Morning

This breathing exercise will help you envisage your perfect morning. Take a pen and some paper, and find somewhere you can sit and close your eyes.

1 Get comfortable with your breathing, just like you did for the exercise Observe Your Breath on page 10.

2 After a minute, start to regularize your breaths: in for four, hold for four, out for four. Focus on your breath for a moment or two, becoming more relaxed as you do so. Lean into your seat and clear your mind.

3 Visualize your ideal morning, but there's a caveat: this isn't about croissants, massages or private jets — it's about your real life. Ask yourself:

    🍃 *What time would you like to wake up? How much sleep would you like to have had?*

    🍃 *How long do you lie in bed before you pull back the covers?*

    🍃 *How much time would you like to have to get ready?*

🍃 *If you have kids, do you wish they would find their own shoes or have done their homework?*

🍃 *Would it make your life easier if you packed your bag the night before or laid out your clothes ready for the morning?*

🍃 *What do you need? A long hot shower? Coffee? Breakfast?*

4 Once you've visualized your perfect morning, jot down the key elements — you could create a word cloud of your thoughts or make an ideal timetable. Again, don't be afraid to get creative!

Make Time For Yourself

Compare the notes you made about your regular morning routine (see page 20) with your perfect morning (see page 23). I'm willing to bet that the key difference between the two is time.

In fact, the root of almost all stress is the fear of running out of time. Maybe you fear you won't get something done before someone needs it, or you won't be able to jump on the bus before it pulls away, or you'll make the wrong choice and won't be able to reverse it. Even saying goodbye to a friend or loved one makes you realise that the time you spend with them is precious.

Time is something almost all of us could spend more wisely, but the best way to do this is simultaneously obvious and counterintuitive: you need to take some time to make some time.

Now listen: I know making time for yourself might sound selfish, but it's no such thing. It's actually the best way to guarantee a successful, productive day. Understanding yourself is the key to understanding the world around you, and it can lead you to a happier, kinder, more fulfilled life.

The breathing exercise on page 29, Full Breathing, is designed to centre you; to align your mind and body before the day begins. It's derived from the yogic practices of the Full Breathing and the Three Point Breath, and what it really does is give you some time to focus on *you*.

The magic of breathing is at least partly the ability to get in touch with your core self, mindfully taking a few moments to ask yourself what it is you feel, what it is you want and what it is you need. By giving yourself this time, even if it means setting your alarm 10 minutes earlier, you give yourself the gift of beginning the day focussed on your own needs, your own wants and your own feelings. Of course, this exercise isn't a miracle cure, but it might just help.

Find Your Truth

This exercise will allow you to set clear boundaries and help you get through the day in the best possible way. It will allow you to articulate what you want and what you need, and identify the difference between the two. Which, in turn, will make you a better communicator, better friend and better colleague. When you're able to articulate your own wants and needs, it somehow becomes easier to attend to the needs of others. For example, if you're well fed, it's easy to share a feast. It's a little bit like those airplane safety instructions: put on your own oxygen mask before helping those around you.

Breathe deeply, feel the air rush into your own lungs; find your own truth.

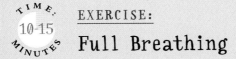

EXERCISE:

Full Breathing

When you first wake up, and before you rise, it's good to stretch your body! (Studies have shown that a good stretch can reduce stress before you've even begun the day, plus it can improve blood flow, flexibility and circulation.)

1 Stretch out each part of your body, starting with the joints of your toes and working your way up through your feet, calves, thighs, bum, lower back, tummy, fingers, hands, elbows, shoulders, neck and even your face.

2 Notice every part of your body, naming each part in your head if it helps.

- *How does each part feel?*

- *How do you feel?*

- *What does your body need?*

3 Notice your breathing too. Notice how it fills your body.

- *Are you breathing deeply?*

- *Where does your breath fill your body? Your abdomen? Your chest? Your throat?*

4 Now, with your eyes closed, breathe only through your nostrils. Breathe in deeply and slowly, all the way down to your lower abdomen. You want to draw your breath down into your body and to let it expand to fill your belly, back and hips. Let the breath expand upward to your torso, between your belly button and the base of your ribs.

5 Next, let the breath come upward again, expanding your lungs from bottom to top, expanding your ribcage and sternum. When you feel your collarbones raise slightly, that's your first full inhale. Congratulations!

6 Now, exhale slowly (still breathing through your nostrils), starting by letting those collarbones drop back down, then letting the ribcage and sternum contract, then the belly. That's your exhale!

7 Continue to inhale and exhale through your nostrils for 5–10 minutes, breathing as slowly and carefully as you can, bringing an awareness to every part of your body.

8 When you're ready, slowly let your breathing return to normal and take a moment to stretch again, noting once more how your body feels.

- *How does each part feel?*

- *How do you feel?*

- *What does your body need?*

- *What do you need from this day ahead?*

- *What do you want from this day ahead?*

9 As your breathing returns to normal, think back to your perfect morning (see page 23). Give yourself permission to take the time to *make* it happen.

Clear the Mind:

9 AM

We live in an age of information overload. It's personal, it's global, it's political, and we're never off duty. Smartphones mean we're essentially on call 24/7: emails ping up night and day, not to mention updates on Twitter, Facebook, WhatsApp and goodness knows what else. We're there for our friends, our family and total strangers on the other side of the world.

Surveys estimate that nearly 90 percent of people under 30 sleep with their smartphone by their bed, and half of the rest of us check our phones when we awake, whenever we wake up. One in ten people is woken up at least once a week by their phone going off and 95 percent of people use their phones right up until they fall asleep[2].

We all have emails in our inbox that need a reply. We all have a text we forgot to answer and now feel like it's too late to respond. And when was the last time you called your gran? We're trapped in an endless cycle of bad feelings and guilt, and it's not helping any of us.

Information Overload

To add insult to injury, this cycle of bad feelings has been monetized: our online world is cluttered with adverts selling us things we never knew we wanted or needed. News clips of the world's apparent imminent demise are bracketed with adverts for luxury cat food, and technology that will run your life better than you can. The only way to cope with the modern world, it seems, is to buy more stuff to help you manage the stuff you're already failing to manage!

Perception vs Reality

According to the news piped onto our phones or tablets 24 hours a day, it seems like the world is going to hell in a handcart. Well, here's the thing: according to many experts, and by many metrics, the world is actually *better* than ever. Global poverty is falling! Infant mortality is falling! World literacy is soaring! More than half of the world's population lives in a free democratic society! These are outstanding achievements.

You see, the problem is our perception of the world. It's impossible to see what's really going on because we're surrounded by bad news. It can even feel selfish and

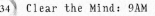

self-absorbed to try to think positively when we're aware
of how hard the world can be for so many. And yet, it's all
we can ever do.

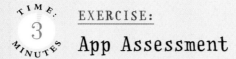

EXERCISE:

App Assessment

This exercise will allow you to take a moment to consider the channels by which information reaches you, and how frequently that information arrives.

1 Jot down or consider these questions:

🥬 *Do you watch the news on television, listen to it on the radio or both?*

🥬 *Do you buy a newspaper or read news online?*

2 You almost certainly have a phone and you probably have at least one email address, maybe more. Consider these questions:

🥬 *Do you have notifications switched on for social media?*

🥬 *Do you have news alerts?*

🥬 *How often does your phone buzz? And how often does it need an immediate response?*

Tip!

There will be a page in
your phone's settings that will
let you see which notifications
you have switched on, and you can
turn them off if you like!

Channel Clearing

By clearing the channels by which information reaches you, you open yourself up to seeing the world more positively and in the frame of mind to make a real difference. Without the clutter and the noise, you'll be able to see more clearly and get stuck into the work that can make the world a better place for yourself and everyone else too.

The breathing exercise on the following page is all about channel clearing – just right for steadying yourself so you can settle down to a day's work. It falls into a class of exercise known as "nostril breathing". The exercise is mainly drawn from the yogic practice of *nadi shodhana*. The Sanskrit word *nadi* means "flow" and *shodhana* means "purification", hence the exercise is called Channel-clearing Breath.

I've suggested this exercise for 9am because it is useful for restoring that sense of calm after, say, a rushed commute on a packed train. Once you've learned the basic principle behind nostril breathing, why not try it any time you feel creatively or physically blocked.

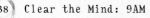

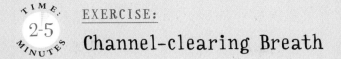

Channel-clearing Breath

This exercise can be done sitting upright and for just a few moments – perfect for clearing the mind in a public setting.

1 Sit comfortably in a chair, with your back as straight as possible. Put your index finger and your middle finger on your forehead, just above your nose. Cover your right nostril with your thumb. Close your mouth.

2 Breathe IN through your open nostril to the count of eight... and OUT through the same nostril to the count of eight.

3 Release your right nostril and cover your left nostril with your fourth finger.

4 Breathe IN through your open nostril to the count of eight... and OUT through the same nostril to the count of eight.

5 Repeat for 12 rounds.

Yoga Coffee:

It's 11am: time for a little biscuit and a big mug of coffee. Whether you call it *fika* like the Swedes, *smoko* like the Aussies or *elevenses* like the Brits, half the globe stops for a caffeine fix midway through the morning. Let's face it, from the fanciest skinny lattes to plain old builder's tea with two sugars, we're a world of caffeine addicts.

Whether you need to wake up or calm down, whether you're having a well-earned reward or an important chat, whether you're holding back a breakdown or building up the reserves to tackle something new, you're almost always doing it with a mug of tea or coffee.

Maybe you've got one on the go right now. I'm even writing this text with one hand and holding a mug of tea in the other. We all do it, and you're probably already braced for what I'm going to say next.

You know it and I know it: none of this is good for us.

EXERCISE:

Caffeine Assessment

This exercise will help you to consider your caffeine intake.

🍂 *How much coffee do you drink a day?*

🍂 *How much tea?*

1 Jot these numbers down somewhere safe, maybe even at the top of this page. Studies have shown that we tend to underestimate our intake of things we think might be "bad" for us, so the results might surprise you!

2 Use the space on pages 44–45 to keep a simple tally of your caffeine intake over the course of a week. Allocate one point for a cup of tea; two points for a cup of coffee (at home) and three points for a cup of coffee from a coffee shop. This point allocation is based on an estimate of how much caffeine is in each of these drinks: there's roughly double the amount of caffeine in a coffee

from a coffee shop than there is in a cup of tea – and *that* contains more than you'd think!

3   Use the space provided in the Caffeine Journal (see pages 44–45) to jot down how you feel immediately after drinking the tea or coffee, and also how you feel an hour later and three hours later.

4   Each evening, give yourself a moment to assess your feelings. Ask yourself:

   🌿 *How does your body feel today?*

   🌿 *How is your heart rate?*

   🌿 *How stressed are you?*

   🌿 *Did you crash or do you feel like crashing?*

Caffeine Journal

Caffeine affects us all differently. Take a few minutes a few times a day to document how it's affecting you and use the space here to record your caffeine intake and caffeine responses.

	INTAKE	RESPONSE
MONDAY		
TUESDAY		
WEDNESDAY		

	INTAKE	RESPONSE
THURSDAY		
FRIDAY		
SATURDAY		
SUNDAY		

The Caffeine Crash

If you're anything like most people, when you review your Caffeine Journal (see page 44) you'll see a correlation between stress, crash and caffeine. You might even, like me, notice a correlation between coffee intake and high levels of disordered thinking, such as panic attacks.

How Caffeine Works

The effects of caffeine vary from person to person, but how it works is always the same. In very simple terms, caffeine works like this: there is a chemical called adenosine that encourages sleep, it builds up in your brain over the course of the day, and when there's enough of it, you fall asleep.

Okay, caffeine blocks the adenosine receptors in your brain. It doesn't stop the adenosine from forming or building up, it simply stops your brain from noticing that you're getting more and more tired. When the caffeine wears off, your regularly scheduled dose of adenosine, *plus* the adenosine that had nowhere to go while the caffeine was blocking your receptors, lands all at once and your brain is hit with a huge wave of tiredness. That's a caffeine crash.

It's easy to understand the temptation to continue consuming caffeine: if stopping drinking coffee is going to lead to a horrible crash, why not just keep going? The answer, of course, is that the crash will come eventually. In fact, mainlining caffeine in this way negates any benefit of drinking it in the first place. Studies have shown that if you're a regular coffee drinker, you're not getting any benefit from your coffee (except the taste).

According to one major study in leading journal *Neuropsychopharmacology*, the feeling of "alertness" that comes with your mid-morning cup is actually "the reversal of the fatiguing effects of acute caffeine withdrawal"[3]. You're not more awake; you're just an addict. You're wearing down your body and mind, you're probably sleeping badly and the crash will come.

So, what can you do about it?

Be Realistic

Now, you're not going to give up caffeine altogether. You know that and I know that, and there's no point pretending. There's no point setting goals you can't reach, and there's no point deciding you're going to give up all caffeine right this minute. You'll manage for a couple of hours – maybe even a day – and then you'll feel a bit tired or need a reward and a coffee shop will be *right there*. And then you'll give up.

This book is all about incorporating better living into the everyday in small and achievable ways. It's not about being perfect: it's about being just a little bit better.

Setting unachievable goals helps nobody. What we're going to try instead is to replace just *one* of those caffeine breaks with something better: so-called "yoga coffee", a breathing exercise that has the same stimulating effects as that first gulp of java. It's also free – and has none of the side-effects! It's partly based on an exercise called *bhastrika*, or "bellows breath", and we're going to try it on the following page, right now.

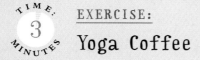

TIME: 3 MINUTES

EXERCISE:

Yoga Coffee

You'll need to stand up for this exercise, so you might want to find somewhere quiet.

1 Stand with your arms resting by your sides. Make sure your back is straight. Imagine a piece of string running down from the back of your skull to between your heels. Is it straight and taut?

2 Breathe normally for a few seconds, noticing the inhale and exhale.

3 Then, inhale forcefully through your nostrils for a count of four, bringing the air *down* to your belly, swinging your arms *up* above your head as you do so (keep them straight!).

4 Exhale equally forcefully for a count of four, lowering your arms back down by your sides.

5 Repeat the inhale and exhale for 2 minutes, focussing entirely on your breath and the movement of the air in and out of your belly, and of your arms through the air.

Beat Stress with Breathing:

1:42 PM

If you've looked at the titles of the chapters in this book, there's probably something you've been wondering. Why, when all the other chapters come in at nice round times of day, is this chapter geared to 1:42pm?

There's a very simple answer: studies have shown that 1.42pm is (apparently) the most stressful minute of the day. Especially on Tuesdays.

Now, this is the kind of thing that's really hard to measure accurately. One study puts the most stressful minute at 11.45am, for example; another gives the vague answer of essentially "between 10:30am and 2:30pm, depending".

But 1.42pm is a nice little number that seems to make sense – you've lost your morning mood, you've eaten your lunch and you've still got ages to go until home time! – and it's as good an excuse as any to talk about managing stress in our daily lives. And, of course, how breathing can help us do that.

What is Stress?

Stress is a buzzword that's used a lot, but what does it mean? Unfortunately, this question doesn't have a simple answer. Rather like the famous description of pornography, "you know it when you see it". We all know how it feels to be stressed, but (according to mental health charity Mind) there's no exact medical definition.

Psychologically, stress is something like a "state of emotional strain resulting from demanding circumstances", but the first definition of the word "stress" in my dictionary is "pressure or tension exerted on a material object". It's actually quite helpful to use this definition to visualize your own stress: the stressors are exerting a practical pressure on your life, like heavy weights on a rubber

sheet. Stress distorts and changes you, pulls you out of shape in weird ways and thins you down.

According to the UK's National Health Service, if you're suffering from stress, you might feel overwhelmed, irritable, anxious or lacking in self-esteem; you might have racing thoughts, be constantly worrying or have difficulty concentrating or making decisions.

The Physical Effects of Stress

Stress is both a physical and a mental problem. Severe stress can affect the body profoundly, both in the short-term, while the stress is ongoing, and in the long-term, as an after-effect.

When you're stressed, your heart beats faster, under "orders" from increased levels of adrenaline, noradrenaline and cortisol. The vessels of the heart dilate and raise your blood pressure. There's even some evidence to suggest that this kind of cardiac pressure can increase cholesterol. Imagine how much harder your body has to work to cope with all of this, thus pushing up your risk of a stroke or heart attack.

And it's not just the heart: stress can upset the respiratory system, especially if you're already prone to asthma attacks or troubled lungs. It's even posited in some studies that stress can trigger dormant asthma – and, anecdotally, it's been suggested that stress can trigger other allergies and intolerances too.

Stress can cause stomach ulcers, heartburn, acid reflux, constipation and diarrhoea; it can increase the glucose level in our bodies and trigger diabetes; it can affect periods, sex drive and even sexual capacity; and it can cause muscular pain, which can manifest as migraines, dental problems or chronic backache. Essentially, there's no area of the body that can't be damaged by untreated long-term stress.

In short, you can't afford to let your stress go ignored.

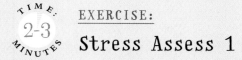

EXERCISE:

Stress Assess 1

Everybody has some measure of stress in their life, whether it be related to work, family, finances, housing or romance. It might be spreadsheets that send you into a frenzy or it could be that having a hundred unread emails makes you panic. You'll know your own crunch points for stress.

1 Take a minute now to think about the things that cause you stress, in preparation for making those crunch points easier to manage and less painful. Are there days that are sometimes worse? Do you find Tuesdays tricky? How do you feel at 1.42pm? What are your triggers for feeling unhappy, worried or anxious? Do you always find a particular person or situation difficult?

2 Jot down your answers – we'll be coming back to them!

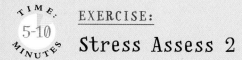

EXERCISE:

Stress Assess 2

In this exercise we're going to assess both long-term and short-term stress.

1 Sit comfortably in a chair (or lie on a bed) and allow yourself to relax.

2 Notice your breathing (see Observe Your Breath on page 10), the inhale and the exhale.

3 Consider your body at rest. How do you feel?

4 Briefly scan your body, starting with your feet and ankles and moving up through your legs, hips, tummy, back, chest, shoulders, arms, hands, neck, face and scalp. Are you holding tension anywhere? Does anything hurt?

5 If you notice any pain, simply acknowledge it and move on, don't try to change anything. Just relax into the chair (or bed), acknowledging your body.

6 Now, consider those stressful moments from the previous exercise (see Stress Assess 1 on page 56). Try to remember how they make you feel physically when they are happening. Does your heart beat faster? Do you breathe more shallowly? Do you feel your muscles constrict or your jaw clench? Do you feel shivery or suddenly hot and flushed?

7 You could jot down some notes when you've finished, if you like. This is an assessment rather than an immediate attempt to change anything – so don't worry at this point about fixing any of the problems.

Two Ways to Tackle Stress

The data you collected in the two Stress Assess exercises (see pages 56 and 57) shows you *when* and *how* you're stressed. Essentially, you've developed a list of causes and symptoms. Now we're going to look at two breathing exercises that you can deploy just before or just after a stress trigger, in order to stop those symptoms right in their tracks.

While you might not be able to do anything about the situations that cause you stress, you can do something about your physical response – and altering your short–term physical response will alter your long–term physical response for the better.

EXERCISE:

Air-conditioner Breath
(Sitkari Pranayama)

Sitkari is said to mean "sipping" or "hissing", and that's a really good thing to keep in mind with this exercise. You are hissing the air through your teeth, to cool and calm the body – the way a sip of cool water does. Properly deployed, this exercise will allow you to be remain cool, calm and collected in the face of (hopefully metaphorical!) fire.

1 Sit comfortably, with your eyes closed. Notice your breath (see Observe Your Breath on page 10) and if you can, start to regulate your breath too. Breathe in through your mouth for the count of four, hold for four, and breathe out through your nose for four. Do this ten times.

2 Now, press your teeth together and draw your lips back as far as they will go, like a kind of cartoon snarl! Imagine you're a cross cat, with your teeth exposed. (This might feel silly, but there's a point to it.) Partly, this redirects your focus from the stress trigger back to the body, grounding you. Partly, it allows you to do a cooling breath that will steady your heart rate, steady your body and even your breathing.

3 Keeping your breathing steady, inhale through the gaps in the teeth for the count of four. Can you hear your breath hissing? The air should feel cool inside your mouth and in your throat, down into your lungs and belly.

4 Relax your lips, close your mouth and exhale through your nose.

5 Repeat for at least 20 breaths, until you can feel your heart rate returning to normal.

EXERCISE:

Cooling Breath (*Sitali Pranayama*)

This cooling, calming breathing exercise is based on an ancient yogic technique. *Sitali* literally means the "cooling breath". To perform this exercise, you need to be able to roll your tongue; an ability determined by your genes. There's no point trying to force yourself to do something impossible, so this exercise is an optional extra. Rolling the tongue, here, is said to mimic a green leaf uncurling or the beak of a bird: these are the kind of cool, natural images that you could visualize once you get the hang of this exercise.

1 Sit comfortably, keeping your back straight, and breathe deeply and firmly for a few minutes.

2 Notice your breath (see Observe Your Breath on page 10) and slowly modify it to become deeper and more profound, pushing the breath right down to your belly and up through your chest. Breathe in through your mouth and out through your nose.

3 Open your mouth into an O-shape. If you can, poke out your tongue and curl it into a U-shape lengthwise. Now, inhale through the curled-up tongue, as if it were a drinking straw! Feel the coolness of the air as it travels through your system. Retract your tongue, close your mouth and exhale through your nose. Repeat for eight breaths. This is the cooling breath.

4 Give yourself eight regular deep breaths and then repeat the cooling breath eight times.

Banish the Commuter Blues:

6 PM

There's something magical about journeys. Or at least, there should be.

Remember what it was like to travel as a kid? The world rushing by the train windows? The thrill of flying? Even walking to school could feel like an adventure: a change in the weather or a change in seasons creating new and extraordinary things to explore and explain, such as dew on the grass or ice on a puddle. Even as a teenager, there was something ultra-cool about sitting on the back seat of the bus with your friends.

I don't know when we lose that sense of wonder – or why. But I expect it's something to do with the way that travelling through the world as an adult is often reduced to taking the shortest route between points A and B: a boring fact of everyday life. How do we get there? How quickly can we do it? And are we running late already? After all, the journey most adults undertake with most regularity is the commute.

The Cost of Commuting

Here's a startling fact: last year people in the UK travelled 801 billion kilometres, of which about 20 percent was for work – that's 160.2 billion kilometres of commuting every year. The average commute in the UK is somewhere between 30 and 46 minutes, and it's even worse in America (perhaps because it's bigger). Someone mathematical could work out how many hours (days? weeks? months?) we're spending, collectively, on the move, but for now, let's just agree it's a lot.

We're trapped into spending a large portion of our precious lives on crowded buses or stuck in traffic or crammed into packed trains with our faces in a stranger's armpit. And while we're travelling, we're trying to make the time count in the only way we remember how: by working on our mobile phones and laptops to make the time pay. It's no wonder that a study from *Psychology Today* found that commuting is one of life's "least enjoyable" activities. It's even been claimed that the length of our commute correlates directly to a decline in psychological wellbeing.

We learned in the previous chapter how stress can affect the body, and if an unhappy commute is contributing to that daily stress, then it's clearly time to do something about it.

Take Back Control

I know what you're thinking: I can't change my commute. And you're probably right. Most likely, you're not going to change your job because you don't like the commute. But this book isn't about what you can't do, but what you can: it's about making small changes that might make a huge difference. So what can you change?

Over the next few pages, you'll find some suggestions for how to make your commute easier and less stressful; making the most of that time in ways that don't involve bellowing apologetically down the phone at your boss. We'll consider what it is about your commute that doesn't work for you – and maybe what does.

But here's the thing, and if you've read this far you'll probably know the gist of what I'm about to say: these changes aren't about changing the environment, per se. After all, it will still be a commute: boring, sweaty, overcrowded and exhausting. What we're really trying to do here is to examine ourselves, and how we react to these situations. We're trying to work out what's within our control and what isn't, and how best to cope with that dichotomy.

Take control of your body, your breath and your experience, and learn to relinquish the rest.

EXERCISE:

The Commuter Blues

1 Take a moment to think about what makes your commute stressful and jot down the answers. Is your it overwhelming, smelly or noisy? Are you always running late? Does sitting for too long hurt your back, or does standing with a heavy bag make you feel lopsided? If you travel by tube or subway, do you spend too much time underground? Do you always arrive at work sweaty and out of breath? Below, I've listed some common commuting complaints, with some easy solutions.

Too noisy

Invest in a pair of noise-cancelling headphones! Audiobooks can be incredibly helpful (you could use this time to catch up on books you've always wanted to read) and podcasts and radio shows, which are often available for free, can

teach you about things you never knew you wanted to know. Focussing on expanding your mind can make you feel like your commute isn't "dead time", and learning something new can be a great way of distracting yourself from overwhelming noise or sounds.

It's also worth trying an app for a crossword or sudoku puzzle: focussing on something small and logical can really help to take your mind off what's going on around you!

Too smelly

A few drops of an essential oil (bergamot or rosemary for clarity; tea tree for freshness) on a handkerchief – like a Victorian lady! – can work wonders to block out unpleasant odours, without being overwhelming for anyone else.

Too uncomfortable

This simple stretch can be
done while sitting, driving or
standing. Begin by noticing
your breathing (see Observe
Your Breath on page 10).
Roll your shoulders back,
first the left, then the right,
then together. Repeat
ten times.

Tip!

Swap your
briefcase for a
back-friendly
rucksack, many
of which are
perfectly office
appropriate!

Too long

Could you give yourself 5 minutes in the fresh air at the
destination end of your journey? Could you park a little
farther away or get off the bus a stop earlier than usual?
A minute or two walking in the fresh air can give you
time to truly reflect on the day ahead, while also letting
you stretch your muscles and cool down.

Focus Your Attention

If you find yourself stuck on your
commute without headphones or
essential oils, paradoxically, it can
sometimes help to be extra
mindful of your situation.
Acknowledge your
breathing and then, like a
dancer doing a pirouette,
focus your mind on one
small fixed point in your
immediate environment
and concentrate on it.
Consider every detail and
really make yourself notice
it. Like doing a sudoku
puzzle or crossword, this
kind of mental absorption can
really help to tone down an
overwhelming environment.

Of course, what we're really talking
is mindfulness, which is at the heart of
all breathing practices, and perhaps at the

core of becoming a better, happier person. Knowing who and where we are is the only way to cope with an increasingly frantic world. This is where breathing comes into it: our breath is, perhaps, the only thing we can ever truly know for certain. It's an intensely private internal experience that transmutes to the universal outside; it's our most fundamental connection to the world around us. Controlling our breathing is, essentially, controlling the world as far as we know it, which allows us to relinquish control of the things that don't matter or are beyond us.

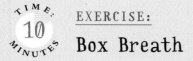

EXERCISE:

Box Breath

This exercise is based on the yogic practice of *samavrtti*, used for The 4-4 Breath (see page 15). This technique is, perhaps unexpectedly, famous for being used by the US Navy SEALs in, let's say, difficult situations with difficult people, which sounds a bit like commuting to me! As ever, it's about regulating your breath, only this time breathing to an even count of four on the inhale, the hold, the exhale and (here's the new part) the emptiness after the exhale.

1 Get as comfortable as you can. Give yourself a moment just to notice your breath (see Observe Your Breath on page 10) and then even it out a little: breathe in for the count of four and out for the count of four.

2 On the exhale, expel all the air from your lungs and count four.

3 Breathe in through your nose for a count of four.

4 Hold the breath, letting it swell your chest, for a count of four.

5 Exhale through your nose for a count of four.

6 Continue breathing in this way for 10 minutes – it will make a real difference to your state of calm.

Home at Last:

It's the end of a(nother) long day: you're finally home and you've completed the responsibilities of the day. This is your time — or at least, it should be.

Too often our evenings become a blur of hurried decompression — and a lot of chores. You never really stop. How often do you find yourself answering emails at eleven o'clock at night, or remembering that the laundry's still in the machine just as you're starting to drift off, or losing two hours reading "nothing" on the internet? How much unwinding do you actually get to do?

You are allowed to have time for yourself, whether that's two hours for an evening class, half an hour with your book or just 10 minutes for a breathing exercise. You are allowed to relax, to want to stop. You are allowed to need that, and you're allowed to want it.

It's easy to know that in theory. However, where's that time supposed to come from? After all, it can seem like our whole life is spent working and organizing and slogging away. But here's something that might surprise you: most people spend about 40 hours a week at work, and if you're sleeping eight hours a night (which you're probably not, but we'll get to that later in this chapter) you're sleeping for 40 hours, Monday to Friday, which leaves 40 hours – an equal amount of time! – for yourself, *plus* weekends.

We have time; it's how we spend it that counts.

How Do You Relax?

Not all relaxation is created equal. Not all "relaxing" activities help us to rest and replenish. Watching telly is fine – but does it make us feel better? Do we feel more awake after watching a repeat of *Friends*? Does the ten o'clock news give us anything new or just more of the same numbing depression that's been drip-fed into our phones all day long? Does mindlessly scrolling through social media help or hinder?

According to a 2012 study[4], two-thirds of people in the UK rely on alcohol to help them "relax" in the evening – a fact that comes with a host of issues way beyond the remit of this book. Does drinking alcohol improve the quality of your sleep? Do you wake from a booze-aided doze feeling refreshed and ready for the day?

You know the answers to all these questions, of course. But have you ever considered what all these things say about our ability to *actually* relax. If we need all these external aids to begin to switch off, what are we missing? And what have we lost?

Learn How to Stop

It seems like relaxing, much like breathing, should be an innate ability. Shouldn't it be obvious how to "chill out"? And yet, somehow, it's never that simple. That's why we lean on telly or drinking or mindless scrolling.

All day long, we're fine-tuning our stress receptors, constantly busy, constantly engaging our flight-or-fight reactions. Our phones fill our lives with 24/7 stress signals, our commutes force us into close proximity with lots of equally stressed people, caffeine hops us up until we crash…

What we're really talking about, of course, is how to *stop*.

Imagine a bus full of people. A bus doesn't jerk to a halt the second the brake is pressed; momentum alone carries it forward for a while. If the brake isn't pressed at the right point (crucially, *before* the bus needs to halt), the bus will sail past its stop, causing chaos for both the people on board and the people waiting – it might even crash. I think you can see where this metaphor is going. It's time for you to learn how to slow down – and when to press the brake.

Of course, that's what we've been doing throughout this book: learning how to apply the brake throughout the day, or even doing so before we even see the stop sign.

Change Your Evening Routine

Assuming you've not yet had a chance to apply everything you've learned in this book, let's give changing your evening – *this* evening – a go.

The next exercise is drawn from the practice of mindfulness. It's called the Full-body Scan, and it's about being in touch with your body, and how it feels. It takes about 20 minutes to do properly – you can find 20 minutes, I promise.

This exercise won't solve all your problems, but it will help you identify them. For this evening at least, it's going to help you consider what you can do for your poor, tired body. And it's going to give you 20 minutes away from booze or the telly or your phone – and I think you'll be amazed by how much better you'll feel.

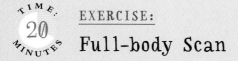

EXERCISE:

Full-body Scan

This exercise is a great way to assess the effects of the day on your body. I find that it can induce an almost trance-like state of relaxation. (Don't worry if you fall asleep!)

1 Lie comfortably on your bed (or sofa) and take deep breaths. Notice your breathing (see Observe Your Breath on page 10), but this time, don't seek to modulate it in any way.

2 Acknowledge and respect your breath. It is what it is. Your day has been what it has been. You are who you are. And all that's okay. You're here now, and you're safe now. For the next 20 minutes at least, the only demand on your attention is you.

2 Notice how you feel, physically and mentally. How does your body feel against the bed? How do you feel about doing this exercise? Do you feel silly or self-indulgent? Is your mind full of thoughts? This isn't about judging, it's about accepting where you are right now, in this moment.

4 How does your breath feel in your throat, your chest, your lungs? Take gentle note of each breath as if it were

the first breath you'd ever taken. Notice your pulse, the way your body rests against itself and the surface of the bed.

5 Now, we're going to draw this close attention into a singular focus: your little toes. How do they feel? Maybe you've never contemplated your little toes before – unless they hurt! – but now you can. Bring your attention into your other toes too: your toes, arches, heels, ankles. How does each part of your body feel? Is there pain or tension? Really concentrate on each sensation, or lack of sensation.

6 Bring your attention very slowly up your legs, through your calves and knees, thighs and hips. This is all you need to do: just concentrate on who you are and how you are right now.

7 Feel your breath move through your body. Feel your attention move up through your feet into your legs,

and from your legs into your torso (back, belly, chest),
noticing any sensations or emotions. You're not trying
to change anything, just noticing and accepting.

8 Your body is worthwhile. You are worthwhile. Your feelings
and sensations are valid and real. Breathe in, breathe out.
Bring your attention to your arms, your muscles, your
elbows, your hands, your fingers and fingertips.

9 Breathe in, breathe out. Move your attention slowly back
up your arms and into your neck, your shoulders, your
throat and chin and cheeks, your mouth, nose, eyes, ears
and scalp. Each part of you is valid. Each part of you
deserves attention.

10 When you're ready, open your eyes and give yourself
a moment or two to notice the world around you:
the light, the atmosphere. How do you feel now?

Getting to Sleep

Sleep is incredibly important for processing, which is a huge factor in reducing stress levels. But like relaxation, sleep can prove to be elusive for many of us. According to one survey[5], about 30 percent of people suffer from sleep problems of one kind or another. So what can we do to change this?

Well, there's hope! If you're one of the third who sleep badly (or even the third who just sleep "okay"), there are things you can do. Let's look at some useful factors to consider.

Caffeine

Could you cut down on pre-bed caffeine? Do you need that last mug of tea at 10pm? Could you switch to green tea, white tea or red bush tea?

Alcohol

While alcohol might seem to aid sleep, it doesn't help you get the kind of sleep you really need. I'd be remiss if I didn't urge you to consider how much you're drinking, whether it's really giving you the help you want, and whether cutting down could be helpful to you.

Screen Time

Blue light, such as the light from a phone screen, interferes with the brain's natural response to daylight hours. It makes the primitive parts of our brain think it's the middle of the day, waking us up and keeping us falsely alert. Try to cut down on your phone usage an hour before bed – and if you can't do a full hour, install an app (like Flux) to soften the light from your screen. Try charging your phone in the kitchen instead of beside your bed, and try to read a good old-fashioned paper book instead!

Sleep Hygiene

Bed should be for sleeping: it's not for watching telly, or working or texting. Getting your brain to associate bed with just sleep allows your lizard brain (the most primitive and instinctive part of the brain) to relax: your bed is a safe place, it's a den.

Sleep Routine

This is another way of teaching your lizard brain that it's safe to relax, just like you'd teach a child or a pet to do something you needed them to do. Simply by giving your brain clear signals that soon the day will be coming to an end (pressing the brake on the bus!), you give yourself a chance to come to a stop when you need and want to, rather than careening on until 4am. Your sleep routine could include a bath, a warm non-caffeinated drink, pyjamas and (perhaps) the practice of the breathing exercise on the next page.

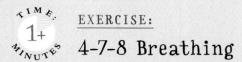

EXERCISE:

4-7-8 Breathing

Devised by an American doctor, and claimed by some to be more effective than a sleeping tablet, the 4–7–8 breathing exercise draws on many of the exercises we've already practised. It's even been claimed that this technique can induce sleep in just 60 seconds[6]!

1 Hop into bed – without your phone or tablet! Switch off the lights and get comfortable.

2 Notice your breathing (see Observe Your Breath on page 10). This time, though, once you're ready to sleep, breathe out all of the air in your body. Whoosh!

3 Press your tongue to the back of your top front teeth – this allows the air to circulate properly.

4 Now, breathe in through your nose to a count of four...

5 Hold the inhale for a count of seven...

6 And breathe out through your mouth in a loud *whoosh* for a count of eight.

7 Repeat until you fall asleep...

Afterword

This little book is supposed to be just about breathing, but you can't write about breathing without writing about life. This book is intended not only as an introduction to the worlds of *pranayama* and mindfulness, but also as a starting point for asking the real questions about your life and how you're living it, helping you to make small changes for the better.

Always remember that you are in charge of you: you matter, you are important and you deserve to take the time you need to consider what you want and how to get it. You deserve to be the best version of yourself you can be; you owe it to the people around you, and you owe it to yourself.

Life is a gift and time is a gift; remember that. Mindful breathing, as practised in this book, simply makes us more aware of that extraordinary fact.

I hope this book is as helpful to read as it has been to write, and I wish you all the best in your continued practice. It's important to note that the exercises in this book are intended as guidelines, and you should always consult a doctor or practitioner in person if you are at all worried or concerned. There are many helpful videos online, many useful podcasts and apps, and many yoga studios that will be glad to help you in person.

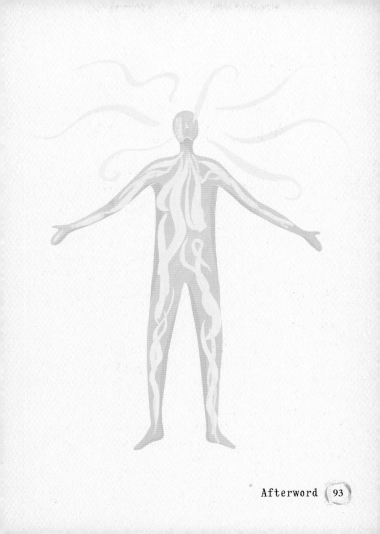

Afterword

References

[1] A 2017 study by mattress company Amerisleep.

[2] Online Psychology Degree, "Getting in Bed with Gadgets: Your Technology is Keeping You Awake", https://admin. mashable.com/wp-content/uploads/2012/11/Getting-in-Bed-with-Gadgets-972px.jpg, accessed 16 October, 2018.

[3] Rogers PJ, Hohoff C, Heatherley SV, et al. "Association of the Anxiogenic and Alerting Effects of Caffeine with *ADORA2A* and *ADORA1* Polymorphisms and Habitual Level of Caffeine Consumption", *Neuropsychopharmacology*, 2010, 35(9), 1973–1983.

[4] BBC News, "Two-thirds 'turn to drink' to Relax in the Evening" (6 July 2012), https://www.bbc.co.uk/news/health-18724115, accessed 16 October, 2018.

[5] NHS Website, "Sleep Problems in the UK Highlighted" (27 January 2011), https://www.nhs.uk/news/lifestyle-and-exercise/sleep-problems-in-the-uk-highlighted/, accessed 16 October, 2018.

[6] Knapton, Sarah, "Simple '4–7–8' Breathing Trick Can Induce Sleep in 60 Seconds", *The Telegraph* (6 May 2015) https://www.telegraph.co.uk/science/2016/03/12/ simple-4-7-8-breathing-trick-can-induce-sleep-in-60- seconds/ accessed 16 October, 2018.

Acknowledgments

I am indebted to my sisters – May, Alice and Hermione – for their love and support with this project; my father, George, and my mother, Ruth.

I would like to thank each and every yoga teacher, therapist and meditation expert who has guided over the years of my practice. I would also like to acknowledge those who have helped me – and those who have let me help them. There is no act of trust like asking for advice, and I am beyond grateful to each of you. Thank you.

I would like to thank my partner for her patience – and I would like to thank our cats in spite of their lack of it.